T0368502

Love Letters
from The Circle of
Life with Animals

*Finding Gratitude and Beauty
in Heartbreak and Grief*

Christin Finn, DVM

Balboa Press books may be ordered through booksellers or by contacting:

Balboa Press
A Division of Hay House
1663 Liberty Drive
Bloomington, IN 47403
www.balboapress.com
844-682-1282

Interior Image Credit: Eileen Sorg, Two Dog Studio

ISBN: 979-8-7652-5703-6 (sc)
ISBN: 979-8-7652-5702-9 (e)

Library of Congress Control Number: 2024923383

Print information available on the last page.

Balboa Press rev. date: 11/21/2024

My deepest gratitude goes to every animal that has crossed my path. From the exuberant to the serious to the shy, my life has been touched by all of you.

I'd like to give a special thank you to all of the owners that I have worked with. Regardless of the nature of our encounter, I have appreciated you.

Contents

Foreword

This book is a precious gem of pure love and compassion!

—Sara Landon

Animals have the extraordinary ability to open our hearts and remind us all of our divine natures and true states of being. As a passionate, lifelong, and devoted animal lover, I can attest that my greatest teachers of pure love have been the animals I have known, loved, and cared for throughout my life. In fact, I simply cannot imagine my life without animals.

Like most animal lovers, each time that I experience the loss of a beloved animal companion, I vow that I will never be able to love again. Yet before long, the emptiness of not having an animal companion becomes unbearable, and I soon welcome a new dog, cat, or horse to the family and to their forever home. Immediately, I am in love again, and although I have a unique place in my heart for each of my beloved animals, my feelings of loss are quickly transformed into love and joy with the addition of a new animal in my life.

I was one of those people who wanted to be a veterinarian from my earliest childhood memory. I loved all animals. However, I couldn't bear the thought of putting an animal to *sleep*, as most people refer to it. I like to refer to it as helping them make their *transition*. I decided on a different career path, but as an animal caregiver, on several occasions, I still faced the difficult decision of helping my animal to transition. It was a moment in life that I always dreaded until something miraculous happened.

As destiny would have it, in 2020, I met my future husband, an equine veterinarian. Even then, I could barely hold back my tears when I knew he was going to put an animal to sleep or when he shared a story of his day, which often included the transition of an animal, until one evening.

My fiancé was on call, which meant he treated any after-hours emergencies or horses at the clinic that evening. Earlier that day, a donkey from a nearby sanctuary was admitted to the vet clinic in serious condition. His name was Big Gus. After dinner, my fiancé received a call that Big Gus was failing quickly and that his owner had decided to put him down. Understandably, Big Gus's owner was heartbroken. She had gone to the clinic to say her goodbyes, but she couldn't bear to watch him being put down.

I am not sure where it came from, but immediately, I jumped up, hustled to the bedroom to change clothes, and grabbed my boots and jacket. My fiancé asked, "What are you doing?"

"I am going with you so I can be with Big Gus when he makes his transition."

"Are you sure you want to do that?" he asked cautiously.

Whatever had come over me was unshakeable. After avoiding and dreading these types of circumstances for as long as I could remember, something was almost *inviting* me to be part of this experience. "I am going," I said.

We both got in the car and headed to the clinic. When we arrived, Big Gus was lying quietly in his stall. He was heavily sedated but alert. I immediately sat by Big Gus's side gently, rubbing his head and adorably ginormous donkey ears. I listened as the staff reviewed his case with my fiancé, who agreed that his condition was incurable and that it was in Big Gus's best interests to be relieved of his pain and discomfort.

My fiancé left with the staff and after a few minutes, entered the stall with a long syringe. He kneeled, gently patted Big Gus, and spoke a few words of adoration to the ole boy. I continued to keep my hands on Big Gus's head but closed my eyes.

In my mind, I told him that he was loved and so handsome. I told him that he was the best boy. I thanked him for allowing me to be with him in that sacred moment. Immediately, I was shown a bright light. I was walking next to Big Gus toward this light. There was no fear but only a deep peace, calmness, and sense of love.

"Go to the light, Big Gus. Go to the light," I said. Then I saw Big Gus walk into the light until there was nothing more to see but that bright light. I knew that he was on the other side and that there was only love and peace there. I opened my eyes and looked down, and Big Gus was gone. Although I had tears in my eyes, I felt no sadness or grief. I felt no loss, although it was apparent that Big Gus was no longer in his body.

For weeks, I thought of Big Gus and the great privilege I'd had to walk with him into the light. I felt such peace and a newfound depth in my own capacity to love. This had indeed been an invitation into a whole new understanding of what our animals experience when they make their transitions.

The experience with Big Gus and many others since changed my life and strengthened my bond and devotion to animals. I now welcome the sacred privilege to be with an animal when it transitions. This book will provide you with a beautiful, expansive, and deeply comforting perspective of our animal companions, their connection to us, and a greater understanding of what they are here to teach and show us if we are willing.

Christin Finn is a hero, friend, and healer to the animals in this book and a steward for the well-being and kindness of all animals. She courageously shares her inspiring stories of the sacred circle of life with animals. This book offers a tremendous opportunity to heal and transform your loss into pure love. It is a gift to all animal lovers during what can understandably be a difficult yet sacred time in their lives and journeys with their beloved animal companions.

Sara Landon, best-selling author and animal lover

A Note to Readers

This is a book about life, the grander plans, growing, and getting close to your soul. There is so much more to the world than there seems to be. If you are open, animals will give you hints to help you know your higher self. You just have to be open.

Even in death—yes in death and dying—and in the sadness and grief of death as we know it, there is so much beauty and grace. And there are many gifts for you here. Just notice the animals. Animals are beautiful guides with so much love. It is not always warm fuzzy love like a soft bunny.

Step back and step forward at the same time. Be open and grateful. Yes, gratitude is a key. This book is here to open your heart. The stories in this book will touch different parts of your soul and spark different memories. It will vary each time you read them.

These are the gifts from the animals. This book is about love and its many facets. You can open your heart while honoring your grief.

The Reality of Life is Life itself,
whose beginning is not in the womb,
and whose ending is not in the grave.
For the years that pass are naught but a moment
in eternal life; and the world of matter and all in it is
but a dream compared to the awakening which we call
the terror of Death.

– Kahlil Gibran

The Circle of Life

These pages are my love letter to all souls. Life is a beautiful circle, starting with coming into this world at birth, to transitioning out of this physical world, and living all the magical and difficult moments in between.

I believe the end of the circle of life is inevitable, heartbreaking, and beautiful. I have found that there is so much love for you here and so many precious gifts and lessons. The passing of your beloved animal is sad, raw, and difficult. But I encourage you to embrace the love and make these experiences as beautiful as they are intended to be, all while honoring the moments when you feel sad.

My chosen profession has given me many experiences in all aspects of the circle of an animal's life. I have been a veterinarian for thirty years. My career has enriched my life in so many ways. Being part of the end of the circle of life for animals has been among my greatest honors.

I hope you will enjoy this book as I share some of the touching stories of my life of serving animals and their dedicated owners. These stories are meant to demonstrate some of the beauty and gifts at the end of the circle of life. There are also a few stories of the gifts and lessons I received from animals in the middle of the circle of their lives. I hope that you can allow the grace of these messages to speak to your heart. I assure you that every single encounter that I have had with an animal has been precious. Your animal's story may not be in this book, but I promise it is in my heart.

From my heart

to yours.

From My Heart to Yours

Many people say, "I wanted to be a veterinarian, but it would have been too hard to put animals to sleep." I, like many veterinarians, would say that painlessly helping animals to complete the circle of their lives is not the hardest part of the job. I consider being with an animal at the end of its life a great privilege and honor. I believe the completing of the circle of a life is a precious, beautiful, and necessary time. Life is, after all, a circle. That is not to say that the end doesn't suck and that it is not heart-wrenching and emotional. It is all those things, but there are many wonderful gifts as well.

My wish for every person is that they can be comforted by the many incredible and precious gifts that are part of the completion of the circle of an animal's life. The words for this book poured out of my heart. My hope is that your heart will be touched by the stories in this book. My goal is that you will be able to see that there is so much love and beauty at the end of the circle of an animal's life.

I will start at my beginning, not at my birth story but at the story of my journey with animals and the end of the circle of a life. I had wanted to be an animal doctor for as long as I could remember. When I was a little girl, I brought home baby or injured animals. My mother explained that I could grow up and become an animal doctor. I never, for a single moment, thought my path would lead anywhere else but to an animal doctor.

At the same time, from a very young age, I had an inquisitiveness and reverence for the end of life. My dear cousin recently reminded me of the funerals we had for bumblebees and butterflies when we were young girls. I had not lost anyone close to me or had experienced any tragedies. But the end of life seemed to hold mysteries that I thought I should know about.

Animals Do Too Go to Heaven!

My first memory of the issue of animals and death was in kindergarten. I went to Catholic school when I was young. I really liked my teacher, Sister Rosa, and I was a well-behaved child. I remember that I had earned stars, which I taped to the top of my desk. These were rewards for good behavior.

One day, we were learning about Adam, Eve, heaven, and hell. I raised my hand and asked, "What about animals going to heaven?"

Sister Rosa emphatically declared, "Animals do not go to heaven!"

I don't remember how many moments it took me, but I stood up in my red-and-gray plaid uniform. I put my hands on my hips and said with all the fury that my five-year-old self could muster, "Animals do too go to heaven!"

A discourse between Sister Rosa and me ensued. I do not remember the details. But I do remember that my mother was called by the principal. Fortunately, my mother was not upset with me. I have no idea what my mother's beliefs about animals and heaven were. But she believed in and supported my passions. For that, I was grateful.

You can be sure that my view on the matter was not dissuaded at all. Of course, animals go to heaven. I liked Sister Rosa, but she was mistaken about animals and heaven.

A Second Grader and a Wake

In second grade, I remember, clear as day, when the nun who was our teacher told our class about a nun in her order—the Cluny sisters—who was killed. I recollect that we were told that her throat had been cut. The sister shared that they were having a wake for her at the convent that night.

I strongly wanted to attend it to show respect for the murdered sister. My mother was an emergency-room nurse. She regularly shared cautionary tales of the ER with me. So she was supportive of my request, and she brought me to the wake.

I remember that I almost passed out when we stepped into a mostly dark chapel in the convent on a hill. The chapel seemed only to be lit by tall candles. I can't say for sure, but my memory is that I could see the wound on her neck. The rest of the wake is a blur. I do have a clear memory of my mom taking me out for German chocolate cake at the La Forge restaurant afterward.

This scenario certainly raises many questions. Why did a nun tell second graders about the wake of a fellow sister? Why did she feel it necessary to tell us that her throat had been cut? You know, I never wondered. It was just one of those Catholic school things. But I knew the wake was important.

The wake was not a class event. I was the only student in the whole K-through-eight school who attended. I did not even think that this was weird either. Like becoming an animal doctor, it was something that I was driven to do.

I have always had a deep reverence for all living things, especially when they have died. I look fondly on my seven-year-old self. I believe that going to that wake was a part of building my relationship with the end of the circle of life. That experience was part of the making of me.

The Day Raven Declared Himself King by Eileen Sorg (Two Dog Studio, www.twodogstudio.com, Eileen Sorg © Copyright)

I Thought It Was a Perfect Solution

I did enjoy Catholic school and the nuns. But there was another memorable episode in third grade. I was at the bus stop in the morning. I found a dead crow. I thought the crow should have a proper burial. I was already two blocks from home, and I didn't want to miss the bus. I came up with what I thought was the perfect solution. I gave my lunch to the dog at the bus stop and put the crow in my lunch bag.

When I got to school, I wanted to make sure the crow stayed safe. We had big pencil boxes that were like cigar boxes. I put the lunch bag with the dead crow in my pencil box and in my desk. It seemed like everything was set. I would bring the crow home at the end of the school day and give him a proper burial.

The plan started to fall apart during first period. The sister announced that there was a terrible smell. I knew the source of the smell right away. I began to sweat. My insides started to churn. The sister proceeded to have every student in the class check their shoes to figure out who had stepped in dog mess. I went along with the exercise and checked my shoes. When no dog mess was found, the nun resumed teaching.

A little bit later, again the sister exclaimed, "What is that smell?" All the boys in the class had to go out into the hallway to get smelled. Mind you, we were all third graders in Catholic school uniforms. How bad could a seven-year-old boy smell? No boy was found to be the source of the smell.

Finally, it was time for recess. I was reluctant to leave the crow unattended. I was very nervous with the burden of my secret. I told one of my friends that I knew the source of the smell. It was my dead crow. Much to my dismay, she immediately ran over to the sister and told her my secret.

The sister came over to me and said, "Give it to me!"

I obliged the angry nun and gave her my crow. I stood alone and defeated as she hurled my crow over some tall bushes by the school building. I remember the wall of the building was yellow. My crow hit the building and slid down the wall. I clearly remember that it was a very windy day. The image of the head portion of her habit blowing in the wind as she hurled my crow was seared into my mind. I was very sad that I could not bury my crow.

I have no memory of the rest of the school day; although, I do remember that my mother was called to come pick me up at the end of the day. I very clearly remember what my mother said to the nun and the principal. My mother, who had deep respect for the nuns, said, "How dare you punish a child who has such reverence for another creature." Thankfully, once again, my mother had my back when it came to animals and heaven.

My heart is warmed as I share these stories of my youth. It seems clear to me that these stories also serve as a love letter to my mother. I imagine that on some level, she knew my soul's purpose. I am grateful that she chose to support my soul.

I Was Nineteen Years Old

When I was nineteen years old, I worked weekends at what was in those days called the dog pound. It was one of the best-run pounds in the country. Their rate of adoption was excellent. It was called the Robert Potter League for Animals. The pound had several very large dog runs. That meant that large dogs needing homes might stay at Potter League for a long time. As you can imagine, that gave us all the opportunity to become very attached to these large dogs.

Even though we took them for daily walks, eventually, these large dogs went cage crazy, and that made them unadoptable. One lanky German shepherd called Esa was with the shelter for over six months. You can imagine how attached we all were to Esa. She was a good girl and was like everyone's pet. But unfortunately, Esa's eventual inconsolable behavior in the run made her unadoptable. The time came for Esa to humanely be put to sleep. It was to be a Monday. Everyone at Potter League was more heartbroken than usual.

I would be working on that Sunday. I came up with an idea. I lived within walking distance to the beach. I could take her home for the evening and next morning. I could take her to run at the beach in the afternoon and on the following morning. The manager said yes to my idea. I did not even think for a second that it would be hard or sad for me. It was not about me. I was determined to give Esa the best last day possible. And I got permission to do that. That made me so grateful.

To this day, I will never forget Esa's joy as we ran at the beautiful, sandy beach in Newport, Rhode Island. She sprinted across the beach with the utter abandon that she had not known in at least six months. We had a brilliant, special time.

Of course, when people commented on how beautiful she was, I told them her story. I said that this beautiful shepherd would be in heaven on the following day unless someone stepped up to adopt her. I had hoped with every person I spoke with that that individual would be moved to adopt her. Sadly, no one stepped up to adopt Esa.

Esa did have an amazing time at the beach, but the inevitable plan had not changed. After our Monday morning beach run, I drove Esa back to the shelter. I did not cry as Esa and I drove back to Potter League. I wanted to stay upbeat for Esa. But as you can imagine, I wailed the whole way home and probably for days; although, you can be sure that I had no regrets. I had only gratitude.

In fact, my tears are soaking the page as I write this forty years later. However, being allowed to take Esa for two beach runs and an overnight stay remains among the most cherished gifts of my life. The experience with Esa brings warmth to my heart all these years later. I know that I was able to bring Esa pure joy. The depth of love and connection that I shared with Esa was invaluable. I would not have traded it for anything. Tears continue to fall on these pages as I feel this connection in the depths of my soul.

Christin Finn, DVM

A Circle, a Hole, and Blessings

Today, the *circle* of life for my dear golden dog Aiven reached completion for him. Something that I want to share is that he lived a fantastic, active, and full life at thirteen-and-a-half years of age. It turned out that despite normal blood work, he had undetected, aggressive heart and kidney tumors.

Two days ago, he barked at the UPS truck, got into the FedEx truck to steal treats, went on an hour-long hike through the woods, and ate a big meat bone. This morning, he enjoyed his daily attempt to steal food from the barn kitties. Then after our joyful, daily, woodland walk, he went into the mudroom and plopped down in an odd location. My heart sank. Something was very wrong. I took him to the Animal ER hospital immediately.

There is an Aiven-shaped hole in my heart. But at the same time, I am so happy that he lived an exceptional life until the end. I would say that he lived full out. In fact, much to my dismay, he stole food out of at least seven clients' cars and five contractors' trucks. I bought a lot of gift cards for people in Aiven's name.

I am sad but grateful and blessed. Today was a planned admin day for me. So I had no frenzy of trying to reschedule clients. Dr. Michael Stone, my dear friend, was working as the ER vet. Dr. Stone made the diagnosis within fifteen minutes. Another gift was that my precious friend Khea had just started working at the ER. She knew Aiven, as she had previously cared for him when I was out of town. And to top it off, the weather was unseasonably beautiful. The sun was radiant. It was a day designed for Aiven and me to complete his circle of life.

I want to share one last thing. I know that things do not always work out this seamlessly. But I want to encourage all of you to please embrace the end of the circle of life with the same appreciation as the middle of the circle. It is all essential and packed with gifts and grace. Don't get me wrong. I am heartbroken but filled with gratitude at the same time.

We All Have That One Dog

We all have one dog that impacts our life like no other. For me, that dog was Iggy. Iggy was a husky-terrier mix when designer breeds were not on purpose. She was a mutt. I loved her with my whole heart. My dad used to describe her as a dog that looked like a bale of straw.

My mom took me to get Iggy when I was ten years old. She quickly became my best friend. No matter what we tried, she managed to escape for a wander almost every day. She always came home, as long as an astute dog officer didn't pick her up first. Iggy had the husky roaming gene. My mom used to say that she was the dog version of me. We were both fiercely independent. In my small harbor town, eventually, the dog officer began to drop her off at our house on his way home.

Iggy was with me for every significant part of my life. She went through my adolescent years with me. We had a paper route. In high school, I hid beer under her doghouse. She was there for all the teenage angst of high school. I cried out my heartaches and dramas with her by my side.

Iggy and I left home when I was eighteen years old. That was a big deal in 1988. I was an eighteen-year-old on her own with a dog. I had to beg and promise my life away when finding places to rent. Luckily, Iggy was an outside dog that hated to be indoors. A carpenter that worked at one of my jobs made her an attractive red doghouse. That doghouse moved with us all over Newport, Rhode Island.

Iggy and I went to college in Rhode Island. Then we drove across the country to go to veterinary school in Minnesota. She went through all the milestones with me. We graduated from veterinary school and moved to western Washington. It was there that Iggy's circle of life would be complete.

Iggy's passing was not a peaceful Hallmark moment. I had just started a new veterinary position. My new boss had gone out of town. I did not know anyone in the town yet. I did not even know where the pet ER was. I knew Iggy had a suspected cancer in her lungs. The specialist in the previous town where we had been living had said that there was nothing that could be done. She was healthy. The mass was discovered by accident. We were due to recheck the radiographs on the following week.

Iggy's decline was sudden and severe. When she started to fail, I was all alone in the world. I needed to put her to sleep because she was suffering. I had to put her to sleep myself. I was on call by myself. Then I immediately needed to go take X-rays of a horse patient and see two more patients after that. I was numb, heartsick, and alone.

I am not sharing this story to make you sad but rather to acknowledge that the end of the circle of life can be really rough and difficult. There are times when it can be very hard to find any grace at all.

Iggy passed away in September. I had her privately cremated. At Christmastime, I brought her ashes home to Newport. I took her to the cliff walk along the ocean. It is where we had gone running every day when I was in college. We lived close enough that Iggy could also safely go on her own almost every day. She had lots of friends that she visited along that three-mile stretch of ocean.

I was twenty-six years old when Iggy died. I was racing through life and was thrilled to be a veterinarian. I was not in the habit of stopping long enough to see all the grace-filled and beautiful moments in life. I do remember how consoled my heart was when Iggy and I went home to release her ashes in the ocean at the cliff walk. For me, it was when she completed her circle of this life.

It is years later as I write this. Now I have the clarity to see the gifts that were in the end of the circle of Iggy's life. For many years, it was a deep wound that I carried. I said that I was alone, but I know that I was never alone. Iggy was always there.

The first day I got Iggy.

The spot where Iggy and I ran every day—the cliff walk
in Newport, Rhode Island where I released her ashes.

The gifts of the circle of life of your beloved animals have no timeline.
You can immerse yourself in gratitude and beauty anytime and forever.

Scan for a video of Dr. Finn and Tonya speaking about how everyday can be a celebration of life.

Tempus Fugit by Eileen Sorg (Two Dog Studio, www.twodogstudio.com, Eileen Sorg © Copyright)

Is It Time?

The time will come when many of you will find yourselves at a crossroads with your beloved pet. You might ask, "How do I know when it is time to let my pet go?" The first thing that I say is that there is no one right answer to that question. It can be very hard to let go of our cherished animal friends. But we must consider the quality of their lives.

At the same time, it is important to consider your quality of life. I have had many clients that stayed up at night or slept on an uncomfortable couch for months. These precious owners spent an inordinate amount of time cleaning up vast amounts of pee and poop in their house from their animals. I have observed that some of the clients have found themselves caught in a vicious cycle with no clear boundaries. My heart goes out to these animal heroes. Some of these clients were just looking for permission to let their animals go. It seems to me that these worn-out owners were judging themselves as not being good enough pet owners. I believe that they needed acknowledgement that they were not bad owners. They were great pet caregivers. I assured them that it was OK to decide that it was time.

I truly believe that pet owners know deep in their hearts when it's the right time to let their beloved ones transition. Please give yourself grace if you find yourself in these times.

I believe it is important to have in-depth conversations with pet owners when their animals are experiencing decline due to age or illness. First off, I want to know how the client is feeling about things. I like to talk about how they believe their animals are doing. Together, we work through any questions that they may have. We speak about what they feel their limits are when caring for their beloved pets.

We'll talk about if they can lift their animals when their animals fall down. Are there stairs that must be navigated by their pets to go outside to potty.

It is my goal for pet owners to be clear and prepared when caring for their declining animals. I have the client identify what defines a good day. I ask what a bad day looks like. You want to make sure that there are more good days than bad days. Owners need to know if they are willing to pick up poop in the house. Many owners are. In theory, I personally am not. There is no right answer. It is just helpful to know ahead of time what your bottom line is.

One of my clients had previously told me there was no way that she was going to pick up poop in her house. Her older shepherd was weakening in his hind end. About six months later, she came in and told me that as it turns out, she was willing to pick up poop in her house. We both chuckled at that. I tell this story to illustrate the fact that you can make a plan and then change your mind. I encourage you to be clear that you are choosing to change your mind.

Sometimes the end of the circle of your animal's life is out of your hands. There may be a fatal trauma or a bleeding event that is secondary to a tumor. While other times, you may be in the position of having to make a heart-wrenching decision.

I have personally experienced both circumstances at the end of the circle of my animals' lives. It is not a matter of one being easier than the other. In these times, despite my sadness, I dig deep and hold love in my heart for my animal and myself. I think about all the love that my animal has brought me. And I am probably crying the whole time. Please be good to yourself and embrace all the moments.

When a Dog Runs Up

Start seeing everything as God, but keep it a secret. Become like the man and woman who are awestruck and nourished listening to a golden nightingale sing in a beautiful foreign language while God, invisible to most, nests upon its tongue. Hafiz, who can you tell in this world that when a dog runs up to you wagging its ecstatic tail, you lean over and whisper in its ear, "Beloved, I am so glad you are happy to see me! Beloved, I am so glad, so very glad you have come!"

—Hafiz

She Was Grabby and Sassy

Over the years, my dear rabbit Ella was our reliable, patient greeter, which found all the dogs interesting. She was never offended by their sometimes-aggressive salutations. She knew she was safe in her giant cage. She gathered many wonderful stories of the dogs that came to greet her.

Ella passed in my arms. Her passing followed six weeks of nursing care for two infected teeth, which were surgically removed by a specialist. During that time, Ella developed gastrointestinal (GI) stasis, which evidently is common in rabbits with any illness. The GI stasis treatment required me to administer subcutaneous fluids, syringe feedings of large volumes of gruel, and multiple medications two times per day.

Ella was a trooper. She continued to eat small amounts from the elaborate buffet of choices that I presented her with each day. She stomped and threw the food choices that she did not prefer. Each morning when I came downstairs, she would hop to greet me and explore what snacks I might have for her. She was grabby with her carrots. Ella was often sassy, whipping the feeding syringe across the floor and stomping her hind foot in protest.

Then she would stop to do one of the most endearing things that rabbits do. Ella would rock back on her haunches, lift her front paws, and groom her face and ears. I never stopped being enchanted as I watched Ella clean her face and ears. I believe there is nothing more precious. When the weather was sunny, I brought her out to the greenhouse. She hopped laps around it and marked everything that she could reach with the scent glands on her chin.

I am, of course, heartbroken. Ella was with me for eight-and-a-half years. I loved and enjoyed her. She was part of my family. I have no regrets that I did my very best, and Ella did her very best. We shared over six weeks of bonding in the house and adventures traveling to various veterinary specialists.

There were many valuable gifts of the journey to the end of the circle with Ella. Amongst these gifts was the inspiration and initiative for me to write about a subject very dear to my heart. That subject was knowing that every day was a gift. The experiences with Ella provided me an opportunity to acknowledge

> Life
> Love
> Beauty
> Humor
> Gratitude
> Connection
> Grace
> Passing with peace

Life is a circle. I hope that people will embrace the end as well as the beginning. That is why I am sharing Ella's story. Our cherished animal friends provide us with precious occasions to appreciate the gifts of the circle of life.

Oakie's Gift

Oakie was a cherished, memorable mare. I did not have contact with Oakie through much of her life, but she made an impression on me that will last forever.

Oakie was short for Oklahoma, where she had come from. She was a three-day-event horse. I knew and worked on her fairly early in my career. Oakie was a beautiful palomino with an admirable work ethic. She came to her owners with a big barbed-wire scar across the front of her upper foreleg. It looked like her foreleg must have almost been cut off by the injury. The clients did not know what the story of the scar was or when she had gotten it.

One warm, sunny day, I was out in the pasture with Oakie's owner and the farrier. The owner and the farrier were speaking, and I lost my focus during the conversation. I was staring off at Oakie as if we were in our own world.

One of the farm dogs was wandering through the pasture. Oakie put her ears back and lunged toward the dog. At the same moment, in my mind's eye, I saw, as clear as day, a dog chasing a very young Oakie into a barbed-wire fence. I stood there breathless; time seemed to stand still. I thought with an absolute knowing, *That's where the scar came from*. I lost all sense of the rest of the world. I made eye contact with Oakie. The scene she had shown me of her earlier life was intense and so real.

I believe that Oakie knew that I always tried my best to care for her, and this gift was her thank you. I felt such an incredibly deep connection with Oakie at that moment. I had indescribable gratitude for that vision. It was a gift from Oakie, which I would carry always.

Oakie introduced me to a special doorway that deepened my soul's growth. It showed me that I could have boundless connections with horses. I will always treasure those intimate moments with Oakie. That experience was pivotal to the way that I moved through life. I was changed forever.

Emmy and the Digging Box

Emmy was a canine force of nature. A friend asked me if I would adopt Emmy because I had two golden retrievers and because Emmy seemed to be mostly golden except for the gregarious part. She was an older stray, which was not mean, but she was not friendly or affectionate. No one wanted her because she was disinterested in normal loving golden retriever behaviors. So I said, "Sure. How hard it can be? I'll take her."

Well, I was wrong. Emmy was quite difficult, but she tried to be good—sort of. At first, I thought she had visual issues because she couldn't catch or follow a bouncing ball. But I could toss her a treat, and she would catch it every time. I was perplexed until I realized that she had no experience with balls; she had never learned how they bounced. I remember the day that I cheered for Emmy when she caught her first ball. Once she figured it out, she was a pro ball catcher.

Emmy had lots of strange behaviors, which I came to believe were from spending a significant amount of time alone. She picked up the largest stone that she could find and frantically ran around with it in her mouth. Then she dropped it on the ground. At which point, she furiously dug around it until the stone tumbled around. The average session took ten minutes. The stone tumbling frenzies were making lots of holes in my yard. I found that quite frustrating, and it made walking in the yard hazardous.

One day when I observed Emmy digging, I thought, *Emmy needs to dig and tumble stones!* So I built a digging box for Emmy. It was five feet square, one foot high, and filled with dirt. My other super well-behaved dogs were instructed that they could never go in Emmy's digging box.

The next time that I saw Emmy doing her stone and digging routine, I excitedly called her name, picked up her stone, and tossed it into her box. She leapt into the box and began digging furiously. Every day, Emmy spent copious amounts of time in her digging box, tumbling her stone. She never dug anywhere else again.

She was a clever dog despite her digging obsession. On a regular basis, she took the other dogs' balls or toys and jumped into her box with them. She knew they wouldn't follow her into the box. Her new prize was safe.

Emmy had another obsession: water. If we were anywhere near water, she would figure out how to get into it. More than once, she escaped from the covered truck—sometimes explosively. Then she ran through the streets until she found the ocean. When I caught up to her, she was swimming. When I went down to the beach to catch her, she swam out into deeper water. In fact, the first time this happened, I was at the beach for two hours. She actually swam across Kingston Bay. I drove a quarter mile to the boat ramp, and she gladly jumped in my car.

After many times of her refusing to get out of the water, I learned to go run errands and then come back to whatever water she was swimming in and call her. If at least thirty minutes had gone by, she came right away and jumped in the car.

Don't get me wrong. Emmy's antics were exhausting. But I loved her spirit. I do think that she tried to be a good girl. She just seemed to look at the world differently than other dogs did.

Once, someone from a nearby property drove up to my house to ask if I could come get my dog out of a pond. I had to be honest. I said, "Probably not, but I'll try." Emmy had gone through my back woods and found my neighbor's pond. I went to the distant neighbor's pond and called Emmy. She just looked at me with disinterest. Eventually, Emmy decided she was done swimming, and we went home. I will never know what previous life experiences led to Emmy's odd behaviors, but I am sure that she made me a better dog owner, a better human, and a more understanding veterinarian.

When the day came that I needed to let Emmy go, she did it her way. I gave her a pre-sedative to make her sleepy. The other golden retrievers and I sat down on the dog beds with Emmy. I gave Emmy a leftover bowl of creamy carrot soup. While she was licking up her soup, I gave her the injection that humanely stops the heart. When the injection was finished, Emmy was still licking her soup and licking, licking, and licking. I said to myself, *What is going on? It was a perfect injection.* Then I said, "Emmy, honey, I think you should be in heaven." She kept licking, licking, and licking until the last speck of soup was gone. Then she sighed deeply and passed. That was a hard experience for me. But my heart smiled a bit knowing that Emmy did it her way.

Years later, Emmy's digging box was turned into a vegetable garden. But it would always be Emmy's digging box.

Enchanting Fierceness

Tulip was a miniature burrow with giant rabbitlike ears. I was completely enchanted by her. She hated me on principle. I found her strong personality so endearing that I made her owners' promise that if anything happened to them, they would leave Tulip to me.

Over the years, I saved Tulip's life more than once. And she grew to hate me more, even though I loved her just as much.

There came a day when a sweet, old pony that the owner's had taken in was scheduled to go to heaven. I can only imagine that this pony had carried many happy children during her life. After the pony had passed peacefully, each of the owner's other horses were brought over to say their goodbyes. Each of the three full-size horses gave the deceased pony a reverent, thoughtful sniff and then walked away. We were all—horse and human alike—in a respectful, solemn mood.

Lastly, Tulip was brought over. Tulip put her head down to smell the pony, grabbed the pony's ear in her teeth, picked up the pony's head, and dropped it with a thump. We all stood aghast for a moment. Then we all burst into chuckling. Tulip gave her final say on the matter. Tulip was a burrow. She was not a person. It was not her duty to be respectful or sad about the passing of the pony.

What I really appreciated about this exchange was that Tulip was able to express herself, and at the same time, she knew where the pony had gone. Through the years, Tulip warmed my heart with her giant ears and precious fierceness.

In Nature, Your Friends Don't Disappear

I feel very strongly on the matter of animals passing and their friends seeing them. In nature, your friends do not disappear. To heal a heart, having closure is an important piece. If people or animals don't know that their friend and family member has passed, it is hard for them to have closure.

Each person and animal has his or her own grieving process. Sometimes with animals, it is an unapparent grieving process. An animal may express a momentary acknowledgement of its deceased friend. While other times, an animal can be significantly impacted by the loss of a friend.

My dog Spring intermittently howled for weeks after his buddy Aiven had passed. He had the opportunity to say goodbye and then to grieve.

What I have observed in my career is that you never know. Sometimes the buddy that was always by an animal's side barely seems to be impacted. Other times, the mare that seems to have hated the deceased horse will stand where she is buried for a month. That is why I feel that we need to give animals the opportunity to see their transitioned housemates and barn mates and go through their process, whatever it is.

And don't forget the grieving process of your cats. As the only wild animal that lets us live with them, you absolutely cannot assume where they stand on transitioned housemates. I feel like cats deserve more discussion, but I am not a cat veterinarian. Truth be told, I am not wise enough to figure out the minds of cats. But I do respect them.

So please, I ask you to do everything that you can to make sure your pets are not left to wonder. More than once, I kept a pet that had passed curled upon a dog bed in one of my clinic's rooms until the owner could come by with their other animals to see it.

Again, I will say that in nature your friends don't disappear. I think there can be many ways to let your living animals know about the other's passing. Sometimes bringing home the collar or blanket that the animal was on when it passed can be enough.

I have a deep admiration for nature. I believe that often, an animal knows when their mates are getting ready to transition; although I think that there are situations when they don't. Knowing that their friend is ready to transition and that they did transition are not the same.

I was speaking about this matter with my dear cousin Tonya. She described a technique where she would create pictures and thoughts in her mind of her deceased animal. Then she would go home and share these images and thoughts with her animals.

But please do not feel guilty if you did not do any of this in the past. There are many unavoidable circumstances where letting your living pets see their deceased friend is not possible. I have no doubt that you did your best and held space for love in your heart. My loving thoughts are with you.

I was very humbled and enchanted by Tonya's words. Speaking with her about this made me want to share it with all of you. Below is a link to a video of Tonya sharing the process of holding space for love and clear pictures of your animals in your mind.

Scan here for a video on creating pictures for your animals.

Conversations with My Dear Cousin Tonya

My cousin Tonya and I are two years apart, and we have been kindred spirits for as long as we can remember. I believe that reincarnation may be a real thing. If that is so, we were pagan, flower-gathering sisters in some lifetime long ago.

I have had recent conversations with Tonya, who lives in a different region from me. I just learned from her that not all veterinarians approach putting animals to sleep in the same way. I feel a little silly and naive for assuming this. Perhaps if I had known that was the case, I would have written this book sooner.

Tonya had the experience of very compassionate vets advising that she not be present for her animals passing. They assured her that they would take care of things, as I am sure that they did. However, Tonya was left to wonder and to have the guilt of abandoning her animals. This did not help her grieving process.

Tonya and I began our conversations regarding my many stories of the end of the circle of life over fifteen years ago. She recently reminded me of a story that I told her about a saddlebred horse dancing and prancing on the fresh grave of his pasture mate. We all knew the saddlebred did not like his pasture mate. Tonya stated that this was one of the many stories that inspired her to remain present for her animals' passing.

The Direct Approach by Eileen Sorg (Two Dog Studio, www.
twodogstudio.com, Eileen Sorg © Copyright

You Cry on the Way Home

The following story was contributed by my dear cousin Tonya.

Woody's Story

When it came time to say goodbye to my twenty-year-old cat, Woody, I knew I had to be there with him. When I arrived at the vet's office, my vet said, "Are you sure you want to stay with him?"

I answered, "I have to." I had always been afraid and too nervous to be there for the passing of my pets. After much contemplation and spiritual growth over the years, I decided to be present at the passing of my pets. I wanted to hold space for them and to comfort them.

My vet gave me time alone with Woody. He made sure that we were both comfortable. During this time, I started to feel a rush of sadness and grief come over me. I knew instantly that I didn't want Woody to sit in that or let that be the last emotion he felt from me. Instead, I brought in the emotion of love and gratitude. It was a process—a back and forth shifting of love and sadness. I realized that it was normal and OK if I couldn't consistently stay in the energy that I wanted. We humans are emotional beings.

I had no idea what to expect next. My vet came in and asked quietly if I was ready. At this point, I was relying on my vet for guidance through the next steps. He was very compassionate. He told me Woody was such a good cat and that he had lived a long, beautiful, and eventful life. We even talked about some of his shenanigans and managed to have a giggle or two.

When the time was right, my vet told me everything he was going to do. I adjusted my emotional self again. I said my goodbyes among the many pets, rubs, and nuzzles. I just held my cat and love in my heart. It was a peaceful passing.

Afterward, I was given as much time as I needed with Woody. I did stay for some time. When I felt ready to leave, I saw and felt that Woody was there with me in spirit. I could feel his presence.

I cried on the way home. I let the sadness come in. I let my emotions have their way.

Later, I reflected on the day. My experience was so much easier to handle than I had thought. I had no guilt. I felt comfort in being able to be there for Woody at the end of his life, after he and I had spent twenty years together. I was there at the beginning, and I was there at the end. Our circle was complete.

I have had many of my pets pass since Woody. It was always sad, and each one was a little different with its own circumstances. Because of my experience with Woody, I will always be there for my pets, loving, supporting, and nurturing them throughout their entire circle of life.

Tonya

Blessing on the Curl of Cat

As Cat curls
In a circle of sun
Sleek and round,
Snug and warm,
A hint of ear
Cocked in readiness
So may I find my place
In the shifting world:
Secure within myself,
Certain of my worth,
Equally willing to
Purr
Or leap.

—Joyce Sidman, *What the Heart Knows*

50

Curious George Becomes King

It had been a normal busy Friday. An unexpected call came in from the Jefferson County Humane Society. The humane officer needed me to check on a goat situation in Port Townsend. I, of course, obliged. I set out this drizzly late afternoon with directions in hand. I had never been to this farm before, and I did not know what to expect. It was never good when the humane society called.

I turned onto the poorly maintained dirt road. This kind of road was commonplace in my practice area. Then I turned onto the property, which had a trailer house in disrepair. There were several dead cars and all sorts of old equipment everywhere.

I got out of my truck and knocked on the trailer's door. What seemed like a hundred small dogs sounded the visitor alarm. When the owner opened the door, the herd of rough-looking little dogs ran everywhere.

I feel that I must take a moment to admit that I was a lot more judgmental in those days. I said to myself, *Holy shit! I am in* Deliverance.

The owner took me to the small building with the sick goat. The shed was dry inside despite the rain. The goat was well bedded with straw.

I was tasked by the humane officer to determine if the owner was fulfilling adequate care of the goat. I was feeling pretty overwhelmed with the situation in general. Thankfully, it was about then that the owner's regular veterinarian, Dr. Richards, arrived. She was a farm vet and far more versed in goat care than I was.

I really just wanted to get off the property. I do remember how kind and nonjudgmental Dr. Richards was with the goat owner. I was impressed with her bedside manner or rather her goat-side manner. Dr. Richards indicated to me that she would handle things from there. *Excellent, I can go.* I gladly left the farm.

It was only in hindsight that I took a moment to appreciate the beautiful humanity of Dr. Richards in that goat shed. That goat call was an adventure. But actually, the real inspiration for this story was what happened afterward. As was often the case, I received another call. The call was from a favorite client of mine with one of my favorite horse patients named Dream. Dream was colicky.

I set out on the thirty-mile drive to Dream's home. There was a bad accident on the highway. I sat on the highway in the dark and in heavy rain for over thirty minutes.

I finally arrived at Dream's home. When I got out of my vehicle, there was a dry, gray kitten at my feet. I didn't see the kitten getting out of my truck. There was no explanation of where he had come from. It was a rainy night. Dream's owners had never seen it before that moment. My truck was an Expedition. I had sat on the highway for thirty minutes. I would have heard him or noticed him. *Did he ride in the under carriage of the vehicle? How could he have survived?*

Oh, yeah, I failed to mention that the goat's property, which I had come from, had cats everywhere. The owners and I both agreed that I had delivered this kitten from an overpopulated, rough situation in Port Townsend to a loving, stable home in Port Angeles. Dream's owners named the kitten Curious George. He earned the name because we all believed that he had explored my vehicle and had somehow hitched a ride thirty miles.

Let's get back to Dream, the reason I was there. His colic was mild, and it resolved quickly from the medicine that I gave him.

Curious George became a beloved family member of Dream's owners. He soon became King George. He became a king when the owners built him an enormous two-story condominium with an elaborate system of walkways.

Through the years, it was notable that King George went into hiding whenever I showed up on the farm. We all thought that he was worried that I might take him back to where he had come from.

That rainy Friday evening, I had set out on two regular veterinary calls. Little did I know that I was to be part of a grander plan. It was my privilege to transport the little gray kitty to his marvelous forever home.

A Time to Talk

When a friend calls to me from the road
And slows his horse to a meaning walk,
I don't stand still and look around
On all the hills I haven't hoed,
And shout from where I am, What is it?
No, not as there is a time to talk.
I thrust my hoe in the mellow ground,
Blade-end up and five feet tall,
And plod: I go up to the stone wall
For a friendly visit.

—Robert Frost

Thank You for Coming

I will never forget that day or that horse. It was a sunny, typical, and busy Wednesday. I know it was Wednesday because that was my day to work in Sequim. I was already in Sequim working on a horse. My office called saying that a horse in Port Townsend was down and that it needed to be put to sleep. I did not know the horse or the owner, but I would never decline to help in a situation like this. It was a forty-minute drive to Port Townsend.

Then my car took me up a small mountain that I had never been to before. I arrived and got my stuff. Then I was directed to where the horse was down. I was in a focused, do-a-good-job mode. With purpose, I took my tote of supplies and walked toward the horse.

The horse was lying completely flat. As I got closer to this horse, which I had never met before, he raised his head and looked over his back at me. He looked right at me, and I swear he said clear as day, "Thank you for coming." Then the horse laid his head back down.

I stopped in my tracks. I am not sure if it was one second or ten that I stood there frozen. It was another one of those moments where the world stood still. The depth of that connection between the horse and me transcended time and nature.

I subtly looked around to see if anyone else looked shocked. No one did. It became clear to me that the extraordinary exchange was between the horse and me alone. It felt like this horse shared a sacred secret with me.

I took a deep breath and gathered myself. I still had to complete the honor of helping this beautiful horse depart from this world for now. The process of helping this new friend onto his next phase went smoothly and quickly; although I walked away a changed person. To this day, twenty years later, the exchange with that horse was one of the most cherished moments of my life.

Blood and Life

Before canine blood banks, when a dog needed a blood transfusion, we veterinarians obtained blood from our own biggest dog. My dog Toby had lots of living blood brothers that we used his blood to save.

Toby was such a cheerful, easy dog to work with. Toby had been a pound dog. I had adopted him from the Portland humane society a few years before that. It was just fortunate or perhaps by a grander design that he was so agreeable to work with. I could actually draw a half liter of blood all by myself.

One weekend when I was working at the emergency hospital, a beautiful yellow Lab needed a blood transfusion to survive. Toby had given blood that week already. Feeling desperate, we called the local pound. We asked the dog officer to bring us the biggest dog they had. We needed to draw some blood to give a dog a transfusion.

The officer brought a ninety-pound brindle-hound-looking dog. We were all relieved to have a source of lifesaving blood. I thanked the officer. That is when he said, "This is a stray we've had for several weeks. Take all the blood you want and then put him to sleep."

I was shocked and appalled. In my mind, I said, *I don't think so. There's not a chance that's happening.* I looked at my technician and said, "Save a life; get a life!"

I brought our precious blood donor to meet the parents of the dog needing the blood. I explained that the big hound was going to save their dog's life and that I needed them to help me make sure that he got a great home. They were so grateful. They definitely wanted to help with that. There was one problem.

Even though their dog was a Labrador, he hated other dogs. But they said that they would call all their friends and local relatives to see if any of them could help this lifesaving dog find a home.

Meanwhile, the hound's blood donation did help us to save the sick dog's life. The hound was a hero!

The hound came home with me while we waited for word on who could give him a forever home. At that time, I lived with my three dogs in a little house on a farm. Don was a friend of the family, who lived in the big house on the farm. Don quickly became enamored with the hound.

The next day Don told me that he started building the hound a doghouse. I couldn't believe it. Don had not been looking for another dog. But he couldn't resist this remarkable dog's need for a home. I was thrilled and relieved. I knew that Don would give the hound an amazing home.

One day later, Don came and took home his new hero hound and named him Roscoe. Don already had a short, red cattle dog named Squirrel. Roscoe was big, and Squirrel was little. When they stood together, Squirrel fit perfectly under Roscoe's belly. The two of them were a one-of-a-kind pair.

It was such a joy to see Roscoe living his wonderful life with Don. I was so blessed to know Roscoe for more than ten years. Yes, that is right; Roscoe lived more than ten years after that fateful day when his blood donation saved not only my patients life but also his own. Who could have imagined that one liter of blood could save two lives? I cherish that I had the experience of deciding to give a death-row hound an opportunity for a fantastic life while he was saving another life.

A Beautiful, Sad, Tragic Gift

I am a person who likes to have a pet rabbit. I have had one pet rabbit or another since I was in junior high. That includes through college and vet school. I remember every precious one of them. To me, a rabbit represents whimsy, quiet peace, and a lot of cuteness.

I have a two-story, octagonal, outdoor rabbit cage that a carpenter helped me build. It sits in the grassy center of my circular driveway. As the centerpiece, this position allows the rabbit to be engaged in all the goings on of the day.

My dogs are always trained to understand that we love our bunny and never go after it. However, I knew and expected that if the rabbit were to run loose in the yard, my dogs' fifty-thousand-year-old wolf brains would be triggered, and they would chase and kill the rabbit before they even realized it was our bunny, which we love.

I assume that you probably know where this story is going. You are likely thinking, *What is wrong with this woman? Why would she share a tragic bunny story?* But stick with me. The theme of this book is the gifts of the end of the circle of life, no matter how heartbreaking.

One evening, I went into the mudroom to give the dogs their bedtime snuggles. I was stunned to see that my ninety-pound golden-retriever mix and my seventy-pound Malinois had stuffed themselves into one crate and that they were basically lying on top of each other. These dogs never cuddled or even slept on the same bed.

I stood there in wonderment, trying to figure out what was going on. The dogs looked nervous and reticent. I kept a big, flat bed next to the crate, which one of them usually lay on. Then my eyes shifted to that big, flat bed. My heart sank. My rabbit Positano was stretched out in the center of the bed. He was clearly deceased, lying in the center of the bed, clean and tidy.

Time moved slowly as I tried to figure out what could have happened. I was in a speechless state of shock as I tried to make sense of the scene before me. *Did a malevolent intruder come and kill my rabbit and lay him on the dog's bed? Could it have been the dogs? How could the dogs have so carefully placed Positano on the bed?* His fur was not wet or ruffled, and there was no blood. He actually looked peaceful. I, of course, was heartbroken and sick to my stomach. Although I was numb, I was grateful that my rabbit had not been mauled or worse.

I picked Positano up so that I could hold and hug him. My heart ached. At that time, I realized that his spine had been broken. That meant that he did not suffer. He would have gone into immediate shock and died instantly.

The dogs spent the entire evening on top of each other in the crate, even though they were free to get out at any time. In the morning, I found that the floor of Positano's cage had developed a small hole, which he apparently squeezed out of to escape—probably to eat some fresh spring grass.

Even as I write this more than two years later, I am sad and queasy as I think of Positano's untimely departure from our family. While at the same time, I am grateful for the incredible gift from my dogs. They clearly groomed Positano before they put him to bed. There was not a speck of dirt or plant matter on him. He was clearly placed in the center of the bed next to their crate. A person could not have laid Positano to rest in a more honorable manner. I am both in awe and am proud of my dogs' ability to rise above their primal nature and have a precious realization of their mistake. I am so deeply touched by the gift of honor that my dog's showed to Positano.

However, I do not have the heart or the urge to get another rabbit yet. I had a concrete slab professionally poured for when I do decide to move forward with building another rabbit cage. The new cage will have an impenetrable floor. This beautiful, smooth slab also serves as a burial monument for Positano. This tribute and his memory may be enough for the rabbit whimsy and peace in my life. I really loved that rabbit Positano.

Mom, Can I Join Karate?

I don't remember the little boy's name, but he left an indelible impression on me. It was an ordinary day in my equine practice. I was called out to a down, sick pony. I had never been to this client's place before. I was accustomed to having no idea what I was walking into when I went to any down equine. I felt like I walked into an episode of the *Little Rascals*—no parents and a bunch of children. The children were all tending to the pony, who was down in a bed of straw, which the children had pulled together.

One eight- or nine-year-old boy was the pony's owner. The pony was lying down and was unable to rise. After evaluating the pony, it was clear that she needed to be humanely put to sleep. I asked the little boy to go get his mother. His mother came out after a little bit. I explained to Mom what was going on with the pony. I also explained that I needed to put the pony to sleep.

Mom seemed to fade into the background. She did not explain anything to her son, but rather, she left it to me. I sat down next to the pony with the little boy. I explained to the boy that the pony was suffering and was not going to get better. I told him that I needed to help his pony go to heaven so that she did not have any more pain.

In a serious grown-up voice, he said, "How does that work?" I was taken aback. I realized that he needed a better explanation. I proceeded to explain that I was going to give his pony two shots. The first shot was going to make her very sleepy, and then the second shot would make her heart stop beating. Then she would be in heaven. At this point, the boy said, "So you mean you are going to kill her."

I was speechless for a moment. I wasn't sure what to say. I felt incredibly humbled. I looked to his mom, who seemed to step further into the background. I paused, nodded my head, and said, "Yeah."

That seemed to satisfy the boy's understanding of the situation. He said, "OK, go ahead."

I do not have children, so I have no experience with explaining the difficult things to young people. But this little boy seemed like he wanted me to shoot it straight. I gave the pony the two shots. Then I told the boy that his pony was in heaven.

He broke out in loud wailing, hugging the pony for about half a minute. Then he turned to his mom, said, "Mom, can I join karate?" and walked away.

I stood there in wonderment and admiration. That little boy had comforted his sick pony, cried, and then moved on. I am sure that he missed his pony over the following weeks to months, even though he was a beautiful example of living in the moment. I was impressed and humbled by how in the moment that little boy was able to be.

Over the years, I have observed that kind of in-the-moment demeanor from many other children whose animals I have helped to heaven. It reminds me of the amazing quality that animals have to live in the moment.

Fury and Rage

My first call of the day was an end of life for a polo mare in Port Townsend. I turned off my normally loud-playing radio about twenty minutes from the farm. I like to spend the last bit of my drive before an end-of-life call being mindful and grounded. I consider it my sacred duty to facilitate a peaceful, smooth departure for all beloved four-legged friends. Their loved ones will remember the experience forever.

I did not have any idea of what I was walking into that day. I do always strive to accommodate the owner's wishes and processes. When I arrived at the pasture, there were a few extra people, which was common. The owner's nephew was there to play some kind of aboriginal horn. The owner had a very special linen that his mother had been adorned with after she had passed. The owner read a prayerlike poem. Then he poked himself with a knife. Next, he rubbed his fingers in the dirt and then on the mare's head. It was clearly a sacred ceremony.

A gelding, the mare's longtime pasture mate stood quiet and respectful as the owner's ceremony proceeded. I remember thinking that the gelding was just like a perfectly behaved little boy in church. He was not tied, and no one was holding him. He just stood watching. The ceremony was beautiful and spiritual to me. But I certainly felt the sadness and gravity of the loss. I was honored to be a witness to such a beautiful love between the man and his polo horse.

The time came for me to give the injections to painlessly end the mare's life. She departed quickly and smoothly. After a bit, I and the group walked away leaving the deceased mare and the still quiet gelding standing by her.

What was to follow, still to this day, was one of the most impressive, heartbreaking, and unbelievable things that I have ever experienced. The whole group of us had just gotten outside of the fence when the quiet gelding let out a scream-like whinny. He started running, screaming, and pounding the ground. His hooves were like thunder. He galloped in a perfect circle around the whole pasture. He screamed, and his hooves thundered as he ran. The display of sorrow and rage were unmistakable. We all stood speechless.

After some time, the gelding was out of breath. He stopped and stood at the mare's body. The power and magnitude of his emotion was intense. It was clear to all that none of us had the capacity of spirit to console the gelding at the time.

To this day, I feel a visceral response in my body when I think of that gelding and what he couldn't help but express. I had never before—or have I since—witnessed such deep, absolute sorrow from an animal.

I barely have the words to express how truly honored I am to have witnessed such power and raw emotion from a horse. I believe that experience was a portal into the spirit of the animal kingdom, which left an imprint on me for life.

About six to eight months later, I was at a farm on Vashon Island. The client mentioned that she knew the man whose polo mare I had put to sleep. She shared with me that the man had told her that the experience was horrible. That made me sad. I told her that I thought it was incredible, although absolutely heartbreaking. I told her that from my perspective, the day was both deeply sad and incredibly beautiful. We were all privileged to witness the immense power of nature in that gelding.

I hope that someday, I cross paths with the polo horse's owner. We shared the powerful experience of witnessing the raw force, sorrow, and beauty of nature. I would like to think that it might have been meaningful for the owner to know how impacted and honored my life is from that experience.

Franz Marc's Blue Horses

I step into the painting of the four blue horses.
I am not even surprised that I can do this.
One of the horses walks towards me.
His blue nose noses me lightly. I put my arm
over his blue mane, not holding on, just
commingling.
He allows me my pleasure.

—Mary Oliver, *Blue Horses: Poems*

Every Day Has Its Hero—Today's Hero Was Pretty Boy

As I got out of my truck and walked toward the barn, I did not have sadness but rather, resolve. The day was radiant, the sky was clear, and the pastures were like emerald carpets. Mic, the big bay thoroughbred was enjoying his last thirty hours of life moving freely about the lush pasture. It had been one and a half years since Mic had been able to be free out in his pasture. Serious health issues precluded him from eating fresh grass or grazing on his pasture.

Mic had recently become fractious and dangerous, making it absolutely clear that he would not tolerate any more time in the enormous pea-gravel paddock fenced off from his pasture. That is why the difficult decision was made to let Mic go and to help him to heaven. I advised that he spend his last thirty hours roaming freely in his pasture and enjoying the grass.

On that day, despite his lameness, Mic made his handlers follow him about the pasture for over an hour before allowing himself to be haltered. Finally, Mic calmly allowed the handlers to halter him and lead him up closer to the barn. Hitman, his pasture mate of fifteen years, was by his side.

I briefly centered and grounded myself. I needed to be the leader and the stable one for Mic's departure. I have been part of many horse and dog departures. My heart knows the magnitude of honor and responsibility of holding space for the animals and humans at these times.

I walked up to Mic. I took a deep breath and stroked above his eye. I spoke quietly to this big bay horse. I said, "Goodbye, my friend. You will have peace and no more pain. Please depart with grace."

We walked over to the side of the pasture. Hitman followed us and continued to stand by Mic's side. Hitman could be quite a dramatic, hysterical horse when he couldn't see Mic. We were all concerned about how he would handle Mic's departure. The neighboring horse, Pretty Boy, had been brought over to keep Hitman company. Pretty Boy stood by like the solid citizen he was.

I gave Mic the first of two shots. The sedative quickly took effect. Mic was ready for the final shot. I finished giving that final shot. Mic took a deep breath and gracefully and peacefully crumpled to the ground. He was gone. Mic exited with grace and dignity.

My connection with Mic felt stronger at that moment than it ever had in all the years I had known him. Mic behaved in a distinguished manner from the moment I had stroked above his eye and spoke to him. I believe that he understood and heeded my request to depart with grace.

Hitman had been free, watching from fifteen feet away. Pretty Boy stood by his side. Hitman walked over and sniffed Mic. Then Pretty Boy and Hitman walked away together. They stood inches from each other in the paddock. They were nuzzling. We were all so relieved and grateful for the way that Pretty Boy and Hitman were bonding. There were actually three heroes that day: Mic, Hitman, and Pretty Boy!

More on Mic

Days later, I was thinking about Mic. I recollected how I had first met Mic when he was a three-year-old racehorse. I had practiced at a racetrack training center years before. Mic was known as Kataclysmic Wave. To me, he was just one of the training horses that I worked on. It was by happenstance that he retired at four years old to my client's farm.

As the years went by, Mic was a regular patient, which I got to know well. He was not affectionate. But he was agreeable, cooperative, and a good patient to work with. I was always touched by how this big ex-racehorse was so kind and cautious with the woman who owned and loved him.

Now I reflect on this beautiful horse, which I knew for eighteen years. I am honored to have helped him complete his circle of life.

Mic's Gifts Continued

I completed my appointment with Mic on that day he transitioned. As I walked back to my truck, I said, "Pretty Boy was the hero of this day." I took a deep breath and smiled. My heart was so full of love for all of it. At the moment my heart was expanding with the love for all that was around me, I felt incredible inspiration.

I got into my truck and started writing this book. I sat in my truck, furiously writing for over an hour. The words just poured out of my heart. I had talked for years about writing a book of all the beautiful stories of my career with animals. But I had never once actually sat down with the intention of writing. The powerful inspiration that I felt at that moment completely surprised me. It seemed to come out of nowhere. It was the last thing that I had been thinking about that day.

The fact that I started this book, which I talked about for years, that day at Mic's farm leaves me in wonderment. I would never have imagined that Mic would be so linked to my writing of this book. I am left gleeful in the magic of it all. How fantastic is it that there is so much more to the workings of the universe than we can imagine. It is so fun for me to observe the unfolding of a grander plan. I am honored to be part of this journey every day. And how wonderful it is that my path is with animals.

The Grander Plan Continues

Thirty days after Mic transitioned from this world, the phone rang at 8:00 a.m. It was Kevin, my client's farm helper and Pretty Boy's owner. I knew something was very wrong. I held my breath, thinking that it might be Hitman, the client's only surviving horse. There was a pit in my stomach.

Kevin told me it was Pretty Boy. He had gone down, and he could not get up. Something that I did not mention before was that Pretty Boy was thirty-six years old.

I headed out the door, and I was at the farm in thirty minutes. I arrived at the pasture where Pretty Boy was struggling to rise. I immediately focused on alleviating Pretty Boy's suffering. At the same time, my heart ached for Kevin. Pretty Boy had been Kevin's most loyal friend for over thirty-four years. Most of us could only wish to have such a long-standing friendship.

I felt like I was witness to and part of the greater workings or divine intelligence of the universe. I had been deeply inspired by Pretty Boy just thirty days earlier. He had been the hero of the day when I had put Mic to sleep. I was so grateful and honored to be there for pretty Boy that morning.

Kevin explained that several days prior to that, Hitman had decided to aggressively pick on Pretty Boy. Pretty Boy had been the friend that had stepped in to be there when Hitman lost his best friend, Mic. Hitman did not need Pretty Boy's support and company anymore. One could say that Pretty Boy had completed his last valiant mission of being there to support Hitman. Now he was free to move on. I feel very blessed to have played a role in these sacred workings of nature.

And ever has it been known that love knows not
its own depth until the hour of separation.

—Khalil Gibran

Dogs and Trucks

I have learned that many dogs' favorite places are cars or trucks. It is where many dogs are happiest and most comfortable. One of the most iconic pictures is the loyal dog in a man's work truck. For a dog, it is a great way to keep track of its person because most dogs know that their people will eventually return to their vehicles.

I have personally helped at least thirty dogs to transition while in their owners' vehicles. One such a memorable dog was named Dude. Dude was a big yellow Labrador. He belonged to a friend. My friend was a jack-of-all-trades handyman. And you bet, he had a truck. Dude was always in the truck or by my friend's side. Dude was my friend's best friend.

When it was time for Dude to go to heaven, my friend and I drove up a mountain to his Christmas tree farm. It was a place where he and Dude had countless memories. Dude passed from this world in his favorite place with his favorite person.

My friend was of course heartbroken. At the same time, he was grateful to have some solace that Dude passed where he would want to be. Dude was in my friend's arms, in his truck, and at the Christmas tree farm.

I was honored to be part of the expression of love between a man and a dog. I truly believed this was a sacred bond.

Maybe the desire to make something beautiful is the piece of God that is inside each of us.

—Mary Oliver, *Blue Horses: Poems*

My Heartfelt Wish for You

If you wish for your beloved animals to leave this life in a special place, I encourage you to feel justified in trying to make that happen. You may have to search out a farm or horse veterinarian who regularly travels. There are also small animal veterinarians whose practices focus on providing end-of-life care.

The end of the circle of your animal's life is heart-wrenching. I believe that owners should have agency over what the end of the circle for their animals look like. Follow your heart. Do what you can to make it a precious celebration of its life. Don't be afraid to ask the veterinarian for the things that you need so that he or she can be more supportive during this difficult time—more time, time to call a friend or spouse, moving to the floor, a towel, or whatever you need. Every veterinarian, in his or her heart wants to be supportive of you.

Below is a link to a short video where I discuss this matter of feeling empowered to ask for what you need.

Scan for a video from Dr. Finn.

Three Gifts in the Middle of the Circle

Gift 1. Banging on the Wall

I kept hearing banging and kicking coming from a stall behind me. I tried to stay focused on the horse that I was working on in the aisle. It was a busy day at the hunter-jumper barn. I know that it was a Saturday because kids were walking back and forth.

At one point, I glanced over my shoulder and saw a dark horse's head swing up over the top edge of the stall's wall. I just kept working. The banging and kicking of the walls continued. In my mind, I imagined an elephant fighting a tiger in that stall. I finished the first horse. And they brought me another horse to treat. I diligently worked on the second horse while listening to the elephant fighting the tiger.

Finally, I couldn't bear it anymore. I had to ask what was going on in that stall. The barn owner replied, "Oh, that is just her. She is always like that."

I was struck with a deep sense of internal alarm. I thought with concern, *No horse is just like that!* Then I politely asked, "What do you mean that is just her?"

The barn owner explained that the horse was a young mare and that her owner had gone off to college. So she was really no one's horse. The barn owner added, "She's a Linaro baby." I knew Linaro. He was a fine Holsteiner stallion on loan from a famous barn in Germany. My curiosity and concern that something was very wrong grew.

Next, I asked if they could take her out of the stall so that I could see her. They brought her out. I braced myself for an elephant or a tiger. Instead, I was faced with a lovely, dark filly, which stood still and politely greeted me. That only increased my feeling of disturbance. *Something is very wrong*, I thought. The barn owner said that my program would be great for her. Then she asked if I wanted her. By my program, she was referring to a farm where a friend and I rehabilitated recalcitrant show horses. My friend kept a calm, balanced herd of horses. The embittered show horses would relax and heal just by being integrated into the herd.

I stood looking at this disillusioned, dark filly. I thought, *I have no budget for this horse. And I don't need another project.* I didn't think anyone was cruel to this filly. Her basic needs for food, water, and shelter were being met. Nevertheless, this filly needed something. I felt like I had come across a crime against nature and needed to intercede.

Two days later, I returned to that barn with a horse trailer. I brought a friend because I was concerned that it might be an event to get the filly loaded into the trailer. I wondered which one she would be—an elephant or a tiger. The barn owner walked her over to the trailer. I opened the trailer door, and she immediately leaped in without event. I shut the trailer door, and we drove home.

My plan was to behaviorally rehabilitate her and sell her within four months. Boy, was I wrong. This filly named May was an angry firecracker. I had brought her to my place where I had three chill geldings. She squealed, struck, and kicked. The geldings did not react at all. I have eighteen acres, so everyone had lots of room and plenty of freedom.

Over the following six months, May made me a better human. If I was impatient, she matched my level of frustration with her own. If I was patient, she really tried to be too. She was afraid and angry with certain activities. May was terrified at the sight of the dressage whip.

Although I had taken May with the idea of a quick turnaround and sale, it became evident that I had a lot to learn on this journey of understanding and healing, which this filly needed. When working with her, I remembered how over the years, many mare owners had told me that a good mare had a strong sense of justice.

May came to enjoy our liberty work in the arena, especially when I played music. She liked Enya, Sara Brightman, and especially the soundtrack from the equine extravaganza *Cavalia*.

Over time, I came to the conclusion that May needed a combination of time to decompress from her frustration and anger and to start all interactions with things and people over again. I approached her as if she were a foal. One day, I had a eureka moment. I looked at her teeth and said, "My gosh, you are still a baby. She still had the baby teeth that were meant to fall out at four years old.

May was clear that trust had to be gained and that there were to be no shortcuts. We were on horse time.

Currently, I trim her hooves myself with no one handling her. She just stands like a lady. But in the beginning, I brought her into my arena, played music, and did some liberty walking. Then I trimmed one hoof, I gave her a treat, and we were done. My goal was to show her that I would always consider her emotions and state of mind.

Through the years, I have ridden May many miles, on all sorts of trails, and all by ourselves. She especially seems to enjoy swimming under saddle in Puget Sound. However, she will not accept being ridden in an arena.

May took about a year to decompress and for her to let go of all her anger and fears. She revealed that in actuality, she was a kind, wise, grounded, and an affectionate mare. I would like to add that she is also loving.

As I write this, May is out in her run-in shed. I have had her for fourteen years, and I would not sell her for a million dollars. May has taught me

    Humility
    Horse time
    Patience
    Compassion
    Understanding
    Calmness
    Appreciation of a mare's sense of justice

Gift 2. Make a Lot of Money

I thought it would just be a typical prepurchase exam for one of my regular hunter-jumper clients. The horse was a young Dutch gelding. He had been imported from Holland six months earlier for a six-figure price. He did not work out for the owner who had imported him. I was aware that his price had dropped, as did his reputation. I had no attachment to the outcome of the prepurchase exam. I was there to do my job, which was to thoroughly evaluate the horse for health, soundness, and suitability for jumping.

The horse was quiet and well-behaved; although it did not escape me that I could see the whites of his eyes. I knew this meant that he was nervous and tense. His hooves were a mess. He had clearly had lots of recent farrier interventions. He had fungal dermatitis on all four legs, although he presented as a well-quaffed show horse. He had a tidy mane and a shiny coat.

I proceeded with the physical examination. Then I watched him move. He was lame in multiple limbs at a trot. But I took a step back and surveyed this anxious, well-behaved, young, lame horse. That was when it hit me. The horse was perfectly balanced and ideally proportioned in his structure. This was all wrong. I had a surreal moment or two. I thought, *This horse has the makings of a champion. But he's broken!*

I went back into veterinarian mode. I declared to the client, "You cannot buy this horse. He is lame!" I could have never predicted what transpired next. I said with boldness and assurance, "But I am going to buy him, fix him, and make a lot of money." No one could have been more shocked at that statement than I was.

I wasn't looking for a horse. I had no money; let alone the money they were asking for this horse. Also, this horse was a liver chestnut. I had said to someone days before that, "I would never buy a chestnut horse." The world was spinning. I wondered, *What is happening. What am I doing?*

Over the next several days, many things fell into place. Others fell out of place. This big liver chestnut horse became mine. I named him Aspen for the strength and fortitude of a mountain and a tree. My journey with Aspen did not make me any money; however, the experiences that I shared with him were priceless and better than I ever could have imagined.

My horse trainer and all my friends thought that Aspen was too much horse for me. In truth, he was when I got him. But as I said, he was broken. Aspen needed the healing of his body, mind, and spirit.

I brought him to the farm with the herd of horses. Even though he was five years old, he had no experience interacting with other horses. He was a well-bred show horse. He had only lived in a stall in a show barn. He didn't interact with the herd initially. Then one day while I was sitting on his back, he bucked me off and ran over to the herd. That was actually a great sign that he wanted to be with the herd. And I was good at safely landing when bucked off a horse. I came up with a plan that everyone around me thought was stupid. It was a lonely time for me. But I was determined to follow whatever journey Aspen took me on.

Aspen loved only one thing: to eat. I was keeping him at a farm right near the Olympic Mountains' foothills in Sequim, Washington. We could safely walk in hand for hours. So that is what we did. For six months, I hand walked Aspen for miles and miles on what I called eating walks. Along the way, he ate all sorts of grass and bushes. A few times, he found dirt that he really liked to eat. He innately dug up roots with his hooves.

It was such an extraordinary bonding time. Almost every day, I went for a long walk with my fifteen-hundred-pound friend. Most days, we would do some liberty work when we got back. I played music on a little boom box. If Aspen was confused, he would get as close to the music as he could. That made sense to him. I did not make sense to him.

I will never forget the day that I was standing on a big, overturned water tank and taking in the beautiful sight of the Olympic Mountains. Aspen was free, as always, in the arena. He walked over to the tank that I was standing on. He thoughtfully positioned himself parallel to me, as if I was to mount him. I had not been on his back in at least six months. It was an incredible moment. He did not have any tack on. But he just stayed in that position. I took a deep breath and swung my leg over his back. There I was on Aspen's back. He offered this to me. I sat there on his back for a moment. I thought, *Holy moly, Aspen wants me on his back*. After a moment, I swung my other leg over to dismount on the opposite side. I was on cloud nine. Aspen kept standing there. So I got back up on the water tank and mounted him again.

Those moments were incredibly sacred to me. I hadn't even been interacting with him. I was in my own world staring at the mountains. Aspen chose to walk over to me and position himself for me to mount.

It was a pivotal moment in our relationship. Aspen's gesture served as confirmation that I had chosen the right path for him and me. His actions showed me that I had earned his trust. We had an official sealing of the friendship between horse and owner/rider.

Aspen and I continued to do lots of hand walking and liberty work. After that day, he also became a fantastic riding partner. I think that both fate and angels put Aspen in my path.

Photography by Bonnie Block

Gift 3. Test or Gift

I stood in sunny Sedona as I told my friend Enocha that I thought I would come home from my road trip with a dog. "What do you mean?" she asked. I replied that ever since I had planned to leave on my sabbatical, I had a feeling that I would end up with a dog. I shared how for more than a year, I had been trying to find a Malinois that would be a good fit for me and my dogs. I had given up. I figured that maybe when I visited my friend in Idaho, I'd end up with a big farm hound.

Seventy-two hours later, I stood in a sparsely housed neighborhood in Kanab, Utah. I was visiting my good friend Lara. A man drove up in a truck with a Malinois, which was hanging her head out the window. I was feeding my dogs in the driveway of the house where I was staying. The man asked if I knew a lot about dogs. Suspicious of the man, I replied, "Uh, I know a little." He said that he was getting transferred out of the country for his job in forty-eight hours and that he just found out that he couldn't bring the dog with him.

I thought, *Who is this guy?* I said, "Malinois are high-drive dogs. You should call the breed's rescue."

He replied, "She is not high drive; she is a couch potato."

I said to myself, *What is happening. Is this a test or a gift?* I repeated this in my head.

In a fog, I said, "Well, can you take her out of the truck so I can meet her?" He did. Despite the fact that my dogs were tied, the meeting was quite amicable. All tails were wagging. *Gift or test?* kept repeating in my head.

He was leaving the country in forty-eight hours, and I was leaving Utah in forty-eight hours. We agreed to meet that afternoon to walk the dogs in a nearby park. That would allow the dogs to interact while enjoying a walk. All went well on the walk. We agreed to meet again the next day at a different park.

It all felt surreal. I got back in my truck and asked myself, *Is this dog a gift from the universe or a test of whether I will make an irrational, emotional decision? Am I ridiculous for considering taking this dog? Well*, I thought, *I have been wanting a mellow Malinois that would be right for me and my dogs for over a year.*

I decided that it was a gift and that on some random street in Kanab, Utah, the universe delivered me the exact dog that I had been looking for. Forty-eight hours after meeting the man in the street with the Malinois named Malika, I was loading her into my truck and leaving Utah for home.

I drove for twenty-six hours straight. I needed to get home with this new gift. I was not comfortable getting this new dog, which I really didn't know, out of the truck in the dark or staying in a motel. All the three dogs were troopers. Malika rode in a kennel. Winnie and Spring were free in the covered truck. The three dogs had a crash course in getting acquainted.

I am not going to kid you that the gift of Malika didn't have challenges. Malika ate the screen and jumped out the mudroom window, escaped out the roof of the new kennel we built for her, ate the neighbors rat bait, and two weeks later, ate the neighbors' pot.

I learned from Malika every day. She was a good girl. We took nose-work class; she did not enjoy it, but she was well-behaved. She got certified as a therapy dog. She was agreeable, but her face made it clear that she was not a fan of random strangers petting her.

It is almost two years later. We've got our groove together. Malika is a fairly insecure dog with a splash of separation anxiety. She is sweet and quiet, and she tries hard. It has been a process of figuring out what she likes. It took one-and-a-half years for her to show that she liked playing fetch. She drops the ball so that it rolls to your feet. She loves to run and really enjoys going to Home Depot.

She is curled up keeping watch ten feet from me. It is her career of choice. That is fine with me. I have Winnie, a border collie, which is my over-clever, achieving dog. One of the best parts is that like me, Malika likes to sleep in.

Malika is a gift and a test! Who wants a gift that does not challenge you?

As I was wrapping up this book, one day, a client came to my clinic to drop off a urine sample. At the time, I was outside with my dogs Malika and Winnie. She looked at Malika and said, "She hates her name."

I replied, "That's great. I hate it too. It was the name her previous owner gave her. I looked it up. It means *queen* in Arabic." I explained that I hadn't wanted to dethrone her by changing her name.

The next day, I started thinking about a new name for Malika. I also needed to send Esa's story from this book to the Potter League so that they could sign the release form required by the publisher. It hit me all at once. *Holy, moly, her name is to be Esa.* She immediately gave me a look of agreement. Time stood still. I felt my connection with Malika—now Esa—deepen and become lighter and even more joyful.

Wow, talk about a grander plan. Malika even looks like Esa. I am not saying that Malika, the new Esa, is the first Esa reincarnated. But it all does feel like a full circle moment. And just in case you're wondering, I am crying for joy right now. My heart is so full.

Tributes to Our Beloved Pets

I want to share a very special invitation to all grieving dog and horse owners. First, I will share the inspiration for this beautiful platform with you. My beloved dog Spring died suddenly last year when I was out of town. I was totally blindsided. I found myself numb. I was happy to be visiting family, but I didn't know what to do with my emotions.

Luckily, I had my laptop with me. It was full of pictures of Spring. I started to arrange photos and a video of Spring. I even set this new video to music. My heart was aching, but the process of arranging the photos and video was soothing for my numb, broken heart. The process felt so healing. Spring would always be in my heart, but I needed to start navigating my emotions regarding his loss. I was quite surprised at how working on this tribute was like giving and getting a big hug from Spring.

I thought, *I bet that this process may be helpful to other grieving owners who have lost beloved pets.* That was when I got the idea to offer a place on my website where any grieving animal owner could post their tributes to their transitioned animals.

There is *no cost at all.* You do not need to be a client of my practice. As an animal owner, you are a kindred spirit. I want to support you. Your tribute submission does not need to be fancy. It can be a video, one photo, or anything in between. It is fine to submit a tribute from an animal that you lost a long time ago. I will host these tributes on my website. You will have access to view them at any time. If you would like to post a tribute or have any questions, reach out to me at office@finndvm.com.

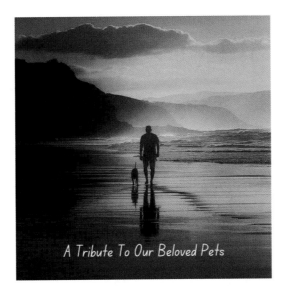

A Tribute To Our Beloved Pets

Please scan here for a video of Dr. Finn talking about pet tributes.

I Couldn't Leave You Yet

I had thought that I had completed the writing of this book, but this morning, I was listening to the beautiful soul that is Adriene Mishler. You may know her from her the YouTube videos "Yoga with Adriene" or her company Find What Feels Good. This morning on her vlog, Adriene shared some beautiful thoughts and quotes that I felt compelled to share with you.

Adrien's site can be found by scanning the below QR code or by visiting fwfg.com.

From the extraordinary book *Autobiography of a Yogi* by Paramahansa Yoganada, I also want to share the following:

After a deep prayer and meditation the devote is in touch with his, her, or their, divine consciousness there is no greater power than that inward protection.

Below is another quote that I found meaningful. *Autobiography of a Yogi* is full of inspiring quotes.

Let my soul smile through my heart and my heart smile through my eyes, that I may scatter rich smiles in sad hearts.

Maybe this moved you and maybe not. No worries. Sometimes we are in the mood for thought-provoking words, and some days we are not so much. As always, be kind to yourself and honor your grief.

Goodbye for Now

My friend, I hope that you were touched by the many beautiful stories of my life with animals and their people. Truth be told, I do hope that you laughed as well as were brought to tears. This book was meant to serve your heart.

From my heart, I hope that your view of death or as I like to refer to it, the end of the circle of life was enhanced. I wish for you that you have the grace to see the love, gifts, and beauty within all the sadness and grief. I want to be clear, in no way am I minimizing the impact of grief. I hope that I have contributed to your life and your animals' lives.

Writing this book was an absolute joy, and it enriched my life. As I wrote this book, I realized that these stories also tell of the making of the person I am today. I hope that you enjoyed reading this book as much as I enjoyed writing it.

Love

To enjoy "Guided Meditation from Tonya" scan for here.

Acknowledgments

I want to extend a special thank-you to a few people whose help and influence was invaluable to me as I wrote this book.

To Sara Landon, thank you for sharing your expansive heart. You inspired me to unapologetically share my whole heart as I wrote this book. Your work gave me the courage to share about the concepts of a grander plan.

Thank you, Carli Christina, for all of your patience, time, and diligence in editing and formatting the art and photos for this work.

I am so honored and grateful to Eileen Sorg for allowing me to include her incredible artwork in this book.

I am truly grateful to Anthony McKuen for his steady nature and meticulous computer assistance.

Printed in the United States
by Baker & Taylor Publisher Services